For Page, Alec, and Jamie

Clarion Books is an imprint of HarperCollins Publishers.

The Bird Book
Text copyright © 2022 by Steve Jenkins and Robin Page
Illustrations copyright © 2022 by Steve Jenkins
All rights reserved. Manufactured in Italy. No part of this book may be used or
reproduced in any manner whatsoever without written permission except in the
case of brief quotations embodied in critical articles and reviews. For information
address HarperCollins Children's Books, a division of HarperCollins Publishers,
195 Broadway, New York, NY 10007.
www.harpercollinschildrens.com

ISBN 978-0-35-832569-7

The artist used torn- and cut-paper collage to create the illustrations for this book.

22 23 24 25 26 RTLO 10 9 8 7 6 5 4 3 2 1

First Edition

The
Bird Book
Steve Jenkins &
Robin Page

CLARION BOOKS

An Imprint of HarperCollinsPublishers

above:
king vulture

right:
Archaeopteryx,
perhaps the first
bird

About 150 million years ago, a small feathered animal launched itself into the air, flapped its wings, and flew away.

It was the first bird.

Today, thousands of different kinds of birds are found all over the world. They have become one of the most successful groups of animals.

There is a bird not much larger than a bumblebee and a bird that stands taller than a grown man. There are birds that eat, sleep, and mate on the wing, spending years in the air without landing. There are birds that use tools, birds that talk, birds that dance, and, of course, birds that sing.

Birds were soaring through the skies when dinosaurs ruled the land and mammals were small, rodent-like creatures. Perhaps the most surprising thing we've learned about birds is this: birds are dinosaurs—the only ones that survived when an asteroid hit the earth 66 million years ago.

But as ancient, intelligent, and adaptable as they are, birds are in trouble. Their numbers have decreased dramatically. Humans are cutting down forests, plowing prairies, and filling marshes—the places where birds feed and nest. A warming climate is threatening their food supply and changing their migration patterns. If we want to help birds survive, we need to learn as much as we can about these remarkable creatures.

A flock of birds

There are more than 10,000 different bird species. They are found in an impressive variety of colors, sizes, and habitats. These birds are shown at the same relative size.

European robin

domestic chicken   shoebill stork   toco toucan   flamingo   great horned owl

black skimmer

broad-billed hummingbird

common swift

scarlet macaw

great blue heron

takahē

eastern brown pelican

What is a bird?

A few birds are flightless—they spend their lives on the ground or in the water. But most birds are at home in the air. Their bodies have evolved special features that have made them masters of the sky.

A bird uses its tail to help it balance when it is perching or walking. In the air, the tail helps the bird steer and provides lift. Some birds also use their tail in mating or territorial displays.

Birds need a light, strong, flexible skeleton to withstand the forces involved in taking off and maneuvering in the air.

Birds use their legs and feet to walk, run, hop, climb, perch, swim, and grab prey.

Many of the bird's bones are hollow, making its skeleton lighter.

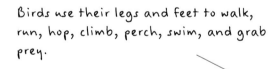

Wings, and their special flight feathers, are what allows a bird to fly. In flightless birds the wings are often small or missing completely.

Most birds have excellent vision and can see a full range of colors, including some that are invisible to humans.

American robin

Teeth and the jaws that hold them are heavy, so birds don't have them. Instead, their beak—also called a bill—is thin, strong, and light. Birds use their beak for feeding, grooming, signaling, nest building, and more.

Birds and mammals are endothermic—they keep their body at a constant temperature. Feathers act as insulation, keeping a bird warm even in freezing weather.

Most birds have four toes. Usually three point forward and one backward. This arrangement works well for gripping a branch or other perch.

Beaks, feet, and feathers

All birds share these features, but their form and function vary depending on where and how a bird lives.

Bird beaks are found in a range of shapes and sizes. Each beak, or bill, is suited to a bird's diet and lifestyle.

This **swordbill hummingbird**'s long, thin beak is perfect for sipping flower nectar.

The **great blue heron** spears fish, frogs, and other small animals with its sharp beak.

The powerful beak of the **Steller's sea eagle** can tear hunks of flesh from rabbits, fish, and other animals.

The **oriental pied hornbill** uses its large bill to pluck fruit and grab small animals. The casque on top of the bill is prominent in males and is used to signal the bird's status to potential mates. The large bill also helps the bird cool down by radiating heat.

perching
The chickadee, like many birds, has one toe that faces backward, allowing it to grip a branch.

running
The ostrich has just two large padded toes. They act as shock absorbers when the ostrich runs.

swimming
Like most waterfowl, the duck has webbed feet for paddling through the water.

grasping
The hawk and other raptors, or birds of prey, have powerful claws with sharp talons that help them grasp their prey.

Birds are the only animals with feathers
Feathers are light, strong, and flexible. Birds have different kinds of feathers, each with its own function.

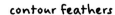

contour feathers
Smaller, soft feathers cover the bird's body and give it its streamlined shape.

flight feathers
These feathers are light, stiff, and flexible, with an interlocking structure that helps in flight.

tail feathers
Most birds have six pairs of tail feathers. They help the bird balance and control its flight, and are sometimes used for mating displays.

down
Lightweight feathers that lie close to a bird's body and help keep it warm.

Bird senses

Like humans, birds experience the world through sight, sound, smell, touch, and taste. But birds have other, more unusual abilities.

The eyes of the **European robin** can sense the earth's magnetic field, an ability that helps the bird find its way as it migrates.

Most birds rely on vision more than any other sense, and birds of prey have the keenest eyes of all. The **red-tailed hawk**'s eyesight is seven or eight times more powerful than a human's. It can also see ultraviolet light, which is undetectable by human eyes.

Many hawks, eagles, and other raptors can spot a rabbit from a mile (1.6 kilometers) away.

The **oilbird** roosts in caves, where the whiskers on its face help it feel its way in the dark. More unusual is this bird's ability to echolocate. Like a bat, it navigates in darkness by making sounds and listening for their echoes.

The **great horned owl** has excellent hearing—it can detect the quiet rustling of a mouse on the forest floor. With its large eyes, the owl can spot its prey in almost total darkness.

For most birds, smell and taste are the least developed senses. But the **kiwi**, a flightless bird with poor eyesight, has a keen sense of smell. Its nostrils are placed at the end of its beak, helping the kiwi find worms and grubs in the litter of the forest floor.

Flight

The first birds took to the air millions of years ago. Since then they've become the earth's fastest, highest-flying, most agile, and most impressive long-distance fliers.

Insects began to fly about 350 million years ago.

Giant flying reptiles—pterosaurs—were airborne more than 200 million years ago. They died out with the dinosaurs 66 million years ago.

Bats were latecomers, evolving flight around 50 million years ago.

eastern bluebird

Flight offers birds many advantages. They can escape danger, find food and mates over a wider area, and migrate to places with a more favorable climate.

Being able to fly comes with some significant costs. Flight requires a lot of energy—birds have to find and eat a lot of food. It also requires a lightweight body and other special adaptations.

hovering

Hummingbirds can hover, fly backward, and even fly upside down. They also have the fastest wingbeats: up to 90 times per second.

flapping

This is the most common kind of bird flight, though wingbeat speed varies. The vulture flaps its wings only about once a second. Small songbirds can have wingbeats of more than 25 times per second.

soaring

Eagles and many other large birds can soar on rising air currents, gliding for hours without flapping their wings.

Oviraptor lived 75 million years ago. It was about the size of a large dog. It had feathers, but could not fly.

Dinosaurs grew feathers millions of years before they could fly. Feathers kept them warm, and may have been displayed to signal mates or warn off rivals. Feathered dinosaurs probably took short, gliding hops as they chased prey or escaped predators. Eventually, some dinosaurs developed the ability to fly.

The **common swift** is a fast, graceful flier. How do its wings keep it airborne?

cross section of a bird's wing

A bird's wing, like the wing of an airplane, creates lift as air moves over it. The air moving above the wing travels farther—and faster—than the air passing below it. This creates lower pressure above the wing, which is pushed up, or lifted, by the higher air pressure below.

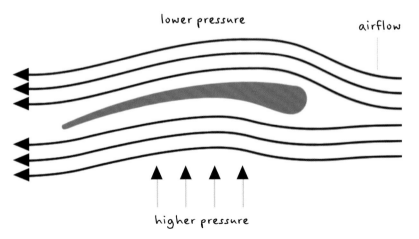

lower pressure

airflow

higher pressure

Becoming a bird

The transition from early lizard-like dinosaurs to the first feathered birds was a gradual one that took place over about 70 million years.

A surprising fact: **Chickens** and ostriches are the closest living relatives of *Tyrannosaurus rex*.

Sinornithosaurus
a feathered, flightless dinosaur

Archaeopteryx
a flying dinosaur, and one of the first birds

house wren
a modern bird

ancient giants

terror bird
A top predator, this flightless bird became extinct two and a half million years ago.

teratorn
Probably the largest bird to ever fly, it died out about six million years ago.

moa
Another flightless giant. It was hunted to extinction by humans about 600 years ago.

These huge birds are shown at the same scale as an adult human.

Bird brain

Our feathered friends have a reputation for being simpleminded. This may be true for some birds. But others—especially crows, ravens, and parrots—appear to be as intelligent in many ways as chimpanzees, gorillas, or three-year-old children.

The **green heron** drops a crumb of bread, an insect, or a feather on the water's surface. It's using these things as bait. When a fish investigates, the heron gets a meal.

The **New Caledonian crow** is among the smartest of all birds. It selects a twig, shapes it with its beak, and uses this tool to extract insects from a tree branch.

Jungle crows in Japan have learned to use automobiles to crack nuts. They perch above a busy intersection and drop a nut onto the road. Soon, if they are lucky, a passing car will crush the nut's hard shell.

But that's not all the crows have learned. It would be dangerous to fly down to get the nut when traffic is zooming past. So the birds wait until the light turns red and the cars stop.

Chickens have more than twenty different calls, each with a specific purpose. If a rooster spots a hawk, it warns nearby hens with an alarm call. But if there is a rival male in the open, the rooster will remain silent, increasing the chances that his competitor will be carried off.

It's well known that parrots can imitate human speech. Some of them actually know what they are saying. Alex, an especially bright **African gray parrot**, could also use tools, count, and solve simple math problems.

Look and listen

Many birds show off their brightly colored feathers. Others perform elaborate dances or sing complex songs. These displays can attract a mate, defend territory, or warn of danger.

Sandhill cranes choose a mate for life. To keep their bond strong, the birds perform a graceful duet every spring.

By inflating a bright red pouch on his throat and making a loud clacking sound with his beak, the male **frigate bird** does his best to interest a female.

The male **satin bowerbird** builds a structure called a bower. He decorates it with feathers, shells, broken glass, and other objects—often blue—to impress a potential mate.

18

The bird song champion is the **brown thrasher**. It can perform more than 1,100 different songs, many of them imitations of other birds.

To attract a female, the male **lyrebird** imitates the calls of other birds, as well as the human-produced sounds of chain saws, car alarms, and more. It also waggles its colorful tail feathers.

The male **pileated woodpecker** makes a loud drumming sound with its beak. This warns other males to stay away.

Nests

Birds need a nest—a safe place to lay their eggs and raise their chicks. They've solved this problem in lots of different ways.

The tiny **Anna's hummingbird** weaves a nest from spider silk, moss, and lichens. The nest above is shown at actual size.

The nests of **cliff swallows** are constructed from hundreds of little balls of mud. The swallows attach their nests to a cliff face or the side of a building, safely out of reach of most threats.

As many as 100 pairs of **sociable weavers** combine their nests into one big structure. This communal nest sometimes gets so heavy that it breaks down the tree supporting it.

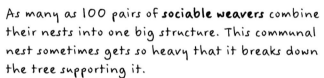

A **megapode** mother lays her eggs in warm volcanic ash. This spares her the task of sitting on the eggs to keep them warm.

Constructed from water plants and anchored by reeds, the **western grebe**'s floating nest can be hard for a predator to reach.

The **flamingo**'s nest is a mound of mud. It's not fancy, but it protects the egg and chick from floods and high tides.

The **Gila woodpecker** excavates its nest in a prickly saguaro cactus, where its eggs and chicks are protected from most predators.

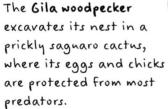

The **white tern** doesn't bother building a nest. It simply balances its egg on a tree branch. This might be a way to avoid the parasites that sometimes infest a nest. If the egg falls off, the tern will quickly lay another.

The perfect package

Bird eggs vary in size, shape, and color. Each egg contains everything a baby bird needs as it grows and finally hatches.

The **ostrich** lays the largest egg of any living bird. The **bee hummingbird**'s egg is the smallest. These two eggs are shown at actual size.

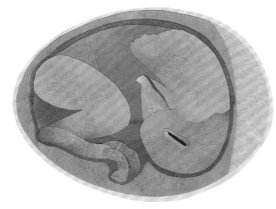

A baby bird inside its egg. It has absorbed most of the egg yolk and will soon hatch.

The **common murre** lays its eggs on rocky cliffside ledges. The egg's shape causes it to roll in a circle so it doesn't fall off.

Plovers lay their eggs in a small depression on open ground. Their mottled shells make them look like rocks and hide them from predators.

A special egg tooth on the chick's beak helps it chip its way out of its egg. The tooth will fall off soon after the chick hatches.

Some birds are born without feathers. Their eyes are closed, and they must be fed and protected by their parents. This newborn **scarlet macaw** won't leave the nest for seven or eight weeks.

Other birds are born fully feathered and ready to go. A **maleo** chick doesn't need its parents' help. It can fly within 24 hours of hatching.

As soon as an **emperor penguin** mother lays her egg, she rolls it onto the father's feet to keep it warm. He'll protect the egg, standing in the freezing winter temperatures of Antarctica for 60 days or more. He doesn't eat or drink during that time. Meanwhile, the mother treks as far as 75 miles (121 kilometers) to the sea to bring back food for her mate and baby.

23

Bird predators

Some birds are vegetarians, feeding on seeds, fruit, leaves, and other plant foods. Others are skilled hunters. These birds have many different ways of catching their prey.

The **peregrine falcon** employs a technique called stooping. It dives at terrific speed, striking a pigeon or other bird with such force that its prey is stunned or killed.

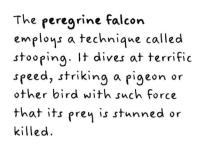

Using its powerful legs and sharp claws, the **secretary bird** stomps its prey to death. It specializes in hunting snakes.

After diving into the ocean and netting a fish with its expandable throat pouch, an **American white pelican** swallows its meal headfirst.

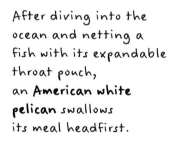

The **common swift** is a fast, acrobatic flier. It feeds on the wing, snatching flying insects out of the air. A single swift can consume thousands of mosquitoes in a day.

How does a hungry **golden eagle** break open a turtle's hard shell? By lifting the unfortunate reptile into the air and dropping it on rocks or concrete.

With its excellent hearing, the **barred owl** can pinpoint the sound of its prey even in total darkness. Owl feathers have a downy fringe that muffles the sound of its wings, allowing the owl to surprise its prey.

Bird defenses

Birds often escape danger by taking flight or running away. But not always. Some birds have other ways of defending themselves.

European roller chicks protect themselves from a predator—often another bird—by throwing up on their attacker.

These **crows** are flocking together to drive away a hawk. This defense, called mobbing, is common among mockingbirds, jays, and other birds that live in groups.

The **potoo** is active at night. During the day, it poses with its eyes almost closed, looking very much like a piece of dead wood.

A diet of toxic beetles makes the skin and feathers of the **hooded pitohui** poisonous. Its bright colors warn predators to beware.

The **hoopoe**, like the skunk, has a gland that produces a smelly liquid. The bird rubs this disgusting substance all over its body, and most predators lose their appetite when they get a whiff of it.

During what is called swooping season, the **Australian magpie** will attack any animal—or person—that strays too close to its nest. Some people wear protective helmets when they are around these aggressive birds.

Burrowing owls nest in underground tunnels dug by prairie dogs or other animals. Young owls protect themselves by imitating the hissing sound of a rattlesnake. This is an effective defense—unless the attacker happens to be a rattlesnake.

To lure a fox or other predator away from its nest, the **killdeer** puts on quite an act. It flops around as if its wing is broken.

Grounded

There are about 60 species of birds that cannot fly. Some, like the ostrich, are large, fast runners that can defend themselves with a powerful kick or vicious peck. Other smaller flightless birds are defenseless and shy.

The flightless **steamer duck** is an extremely aggressive bird, perhaps because it is unable to escape danger by flying away.

The **takahē** lives in New Zealand, where it had few enemies before human explorers arrived with dogs, rats, and other predators. For decades, these birds were thought to be extinct. But in 1948 a few living takahē were discovered. There are now about 400 of them living in the wild.

The **greater rhea** is a large bird, though it is smaller than its relative the ostrich. As it runs, the rhea opens and flaps its wings to help it stay balanced.

Water world

The ocean is a rich source of food, so it makes sense that many birds live on or near the sea. Even birds that spend most of their time in the water come to land to nest and raise their chicks.

The **mallard** is a dabbling duck. It turns upside down to feed on water plants and small animals.

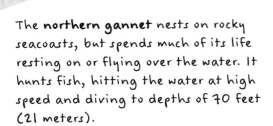

The **northern gannet** nests on rocky seacoasts, but spends much of its life resting on or flying over the water. It hunts fish, hitting the water at high speed and diving to depths of 70 feet (21 meters).

The Humboldt penguin, a fast swimmer, pursues fish and squid. These birds dig their nests in thick deposits of guano—bird poop—that have built up on the shore.

World travelers

Many birds migrate, moving from one place to another on a regular schedule. They travel to find warm weather, a better food supply, or a safe place to nest. These birds can cover great distances, making them world-champion migrators. But how do they find their way?

The sound of a waterfall, the calls of other birds, or the rumble of traffic on a highway can act as a guide.

Many birds have special chemicals in their beak or eyes that allow them to follow lines of force in the earth's magnetic field.

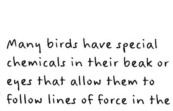

While most birds don't have a highly developed sense of smell, the odors of a marsh, forest, or city can be helpful signposts on a journey.

rock pigeon

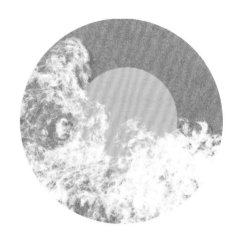

During the day, birds use the position of the sun to help them navigate.

At night, they watch the stars—especially the North Star, which appears to stay in the same place in the sky while other stars move around it.

Birds recognize rivers, mountains, and other geographic features and use them as landmarks.

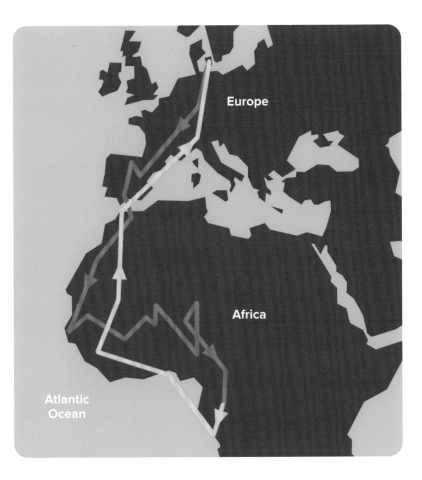

Europe

Africa

Atlantic
Ocean

Scientists attach small, lightweight radio transmitters to migrating birds to find out exactly where they go. The map shows a single **common swift**'s actual route as it migrates south in the fall (orange line) and north in the sping (yellow line).

The **arctic tern** migrates farther than any other animal, flying up to 25,000 miles (40,234 kilometers) every year. It leaves the Arctic in the fall and arrives in Antarctica when summer in the southern hemisphere is beginning. The tern enjoys two summers every year.

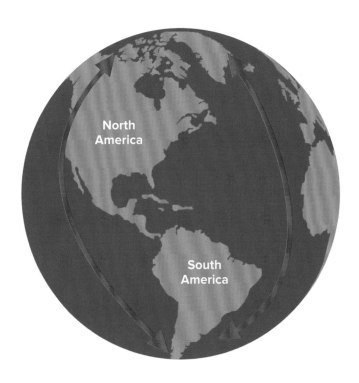

North
America

South
America

Two of the **arctic tern**'s migration routes

Three extraordinary birds

The **marabou stork** stands almost as tall as a grown man. Both males and females have a colorful throat pouch, which they use in mating displays.

The **cassowary** is considered the world's most dangerous bird. It can be aggressive and has huge feet and sharp claws. A kick from this bird has killed adult humans.

where the marabou stork lives

Africa

Atlantic Ocean

where the cassowary lives

Australia

Indian Ocean

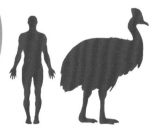

When he's trying to impress a female, the male **red bird of paradise** puts on quite a performance. He spreads and flutters his wings and long black tail feathers, sometimes turning upside down to enhance the effect. These dances can last for hours.

where the red bird of paradise lives

Indonesia

Indian Ocean

Champions

Here are a few of the record holders of the bird world.

smallest

The **bee hummingbird** weighs less than a Ping-Pong ball. It is shown here at actual size.

highest flier

Rüppell's vulture has been spotted flying at an altitude of 37,000 feet (11,278 meters).

deepest diver

The **emperor penguin** can dive to ocean depths of 1,850 feet (564 meters).

multiple records

The **ostrich** is the largest living bird and the fastest running bird. It also lays the largest egg of any bird.

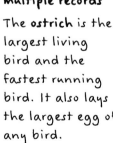

most numerous wild bird

It is estimated that there are one and a half billion **red-billed queleas.**

heaviest flying bird

The **Kori bustard** weighs as much as 40 pounds (18 kilograms). Though it can fly, it spends most of its time on the ground.

most numerous of all

There are about 26 billion **domestic chickens** living on the planet.

largest wingspan

The **wandering albatross** has the largest wingspan of any living bird.

oldest

There are reports of birds living for more than 100 years, but the oldest bird for which we have proof of age was Cookie, a **pink cockatoo** that lived to be 83.

fastest flier

The **peregrine falcon** can reach speeds of 200 mph (322 kph) in a dive.

Birds in danger

All over the world, birds are in danger. As cities, farms, and ranches grow, bird habitats are being destroyed. Many birds are lost to hunting and poaching. Rapid climate change is threatening birds' food supply. And as many as one billion birds are killed every year by colliding with glass buildings. Here are a few of the most endangered birds and the estimated number of individuals still living in the wild.*

kākāpō
200 left in
the wild

northern bald ibis
fewer than 500 left
in the wild

California condor
318 left in
the wild

blue-throated macaw
about 400 left in
the wild

* as of 2022

Gone forever

These birds are extinct.

dodo

This gentle bird became extinct in 1662, mostly due to predation by dogs, rats, and pigs introduced by human settlers.

passenger pigeon

Before they were hunted to extinction for food and sport, these birds numbered in the hundreds of millions. The last passenger pigeon, named Martha, died in the Cincinnati Zoo in 1914.

ivory-billed woodpecker

This bird was last seen in 1944.

elephant bird

The largest bird that ever lived was hunted to extinction by humans around the year 1100.

coming back

By 1941, there were only 21 **whooping cranes** left alive. Today, thanks to protection and breeding programs, there are about 600.

This table shows the size, diet, and range of the birds in this book. Average sizes are given.

	name	size	diet	range
page 2	**king vulture**	length 29 in (74 cm) wingspan 6 ft (183 cm)	carrion (dead animals), garbage	southern Mexico to northern Argentina
pages 3, 15	*Archaeopteryx*	length 20 in (51 cm)	probably small reptiles, amphibians, mammals, insects	what is now southern Germany
pages 4, 14, 17, 35	**domestic chicken**	weight 7 lbs (3 kg)	fruit, vegetables, grains, table scraps	worldwide
pages 4, 10	**European robin**	length 5 in (13 cm)	insects, other invertebrates, seeds, fruit	Europe, western Asia, North Africa
page 4	**shoebill stork**	height 4 ft (122 cm)	fish, reptiles, rodents, small birds	central and eastern Africa
page 4	**toco toucan**	length 2 ft (61 cm)	fruit, insects, frogs, small reptiles, small birds, eggs	northern and central South America
pages 4, 21	**flamingo**	height 53 in (135 cm)	shrimp, seeds, algae, microscopic organisms, mollusks	coastal regions of Europe, western Asia, Africa, the Caribbean, Central and South America
pages 4, 11	**great horned owl**	length 22 in (56 cm)	mammals, birds, snakes, lizards, frogs, insects, scorpions	North America and South America except for rain forests and polar regions
pages 5, 23	**scarlet macaw**	length 32 in (81 cm)	nuts, seeds, leaves, fruit, insects	Central America, northern South America
page 5	**black skimmer**	length 18 in (46 cm)	fish, small crustaceans	eastern coast of the US, South America
pages 5, 8	**great blue heron**	height 50 in (127 cm)	fish, reptiles, amphibians, insects, rodents, birds	North America, Central America, the Caribbean, Galápagos Islands
pages 5, 28	**takahē**	height 25 in (64 cm)	grass, insects	New Zealand
page 5	**broad-billed hummingbird**	length 3½ in (9 cm)	nectar, insects	Mexico, southwestern United States
page 5	**eastern brown pelican**	wingspan 7 ft (213 cm)	fish, crustaceans	coastal regions of the US, the Gulf of Mexico, northern South America
pages 5, 13, 25, 31	**common swift**	length 6½ in (17 cm)	flying insects, spiders, ants	Europe, Asia, and Africa
page 6–7	**American robin**	length 10 in (25 cm)	insects, berries, earthworms	North America
page 8	**swordbill hummingbird**	length 5 in (13 cm)	nectar	Andean regions of South America
page 8	**Steller's sea eagle**	length 37 in (94 cm)	fish, crabs, shellfish, squid, ducks, small animals, gulls, carrion	Pacific coast of northern Asia
page 8	**oriental pied hornbill**	length 23½ in (60cm)	fruit, small animals	India and Southeast Asia
page 10	**red-tailed hawk**	wingspan 4 ft (122 cm)	small mammals, birds, reptiles	North and Central America
page 11	**oilbird**	length 17 in (43 cm)	fruit	northwestern South America, Central America
page 11	**kiwi**	weight 7 lbs (3 kg)	worms, insects, larvae, berries	New Zealand
page 12	**eastern bluebird**	length 7 in (18 cm)	insects, other invertebrates, fruit	eastern North America, Central America
page 13	*Oviraptor*	length 5 ft (1½ m)	probably fruit, eggs, shellfish	what is now Mongolia

	name	size	diet	range
page 14	*Eoraptor*	length 3 ft (91 cm)	omnivorous	what is now Argentina
page 15	*Sinornithosaurus*	length 4 ft (122 cm)	carnivorous, possibly small prey such as birds	what is now China
page 15	**house wren**	length 5 in (13 cm)	insects, spiders, other invertebrates	central Canada to southern South America
page 15	terror bird	height 6 ft (183 cm)	carnivorous	what is now South America
page 15	teratorn	wingspan 11½ ft (3½ m)	carrion, smaller vertebrates	what is now North and South America
page 15	moa	height 10 ft (3 m)	seeds, fruit, leaves, grasses	New Zealand
page 16, 26	**New Caledonian crow**	length 16 in (41 cm)	invertebrates, eggs, nestlings, small mammals, snails, nuts, seeds	New Caledonia
page 16	**green heron**	length 17 in (43 cm)	fish, invertebrates, snakes, small rodents	North and Central America
page 17	**jungle crow**	length 20 in (51 cm)	small mammals, birds, insects, seeds, fruit, garbage, carrion	Asia
page 17	**African gray parrot**	length 13 in (33 cm)	fruit, nuts, seeds	central Africa
page 18	**sandhill crane**	height 3½ ft (1 m)	insects, roots, rodents, frogs, reptiles, baby birds, fruit, seeds	North America, northeastern Siberia, Cuba
page 18	**frigate bird**	length 3¼ ft (99 cm)	small fish, squid, jellyfish, crustaceans	tropical and subtropical waters
page 18	**satin bowerbird**	length 13 in (33 cm)	fruit, leaves, seeds, insects	eastern Australia
page 19	**brown thrasher**	length 11 in (28 cm)	insects, berries, nuts	United States and Canada
page 19	**lyrebird**	length 35 in (89 cm)	insects, other invertebrates	southeastern Australia, Tasmania
page 19	**pileated woodpecker**	length 18 in (46 cm)	ants, other insects, fruit, nuts	United States and Canada
page 20	**Anna's hummingbird**	length 4 in (10 cm)	nectar, insects	western coast of North America
page 20	**cliff swallow**	length 5 in (13 cm)	insects, berries	North and South America
page 20	**sociable weaver**	length 5½ in (14 cm)	insects, seeds	southern Africa
page 20	**megapode**	length 20 in (51 cm)	leaves, seeds, berries, buds, invertebrates	islands of the southwest Pacific
page 21	**western grebe**	length 26 in (66 cm)	fish, crustaceans, insects, worms, salamanders	western North America
page 21	**Gila woodpecker**	length 9 in (23 cm)	insects, fruit	southwestern United States, Mexico
page 21	**white tern**	length 1 ft (30 cm)	small fish, squid, crustaceans	subtropical and tropical South Atlantic, Pacific, and Indian Oceans
pages 22, 34	**ostrich**	height 8 ft (244 cm) weight 250 lbs (113 kg)	seeds, shrubs, grass, fruit, flowers, insects, small reptiles	Africa
pages 22, 34	**bee hummingbird**	length 2¼ in (6 cm)	nectar, insects, spiders	Cuba

	name	size	diet	range
page 22	**common murre**	length 17 in (43 cm)	fish, crustaceans, marine worms, squid	northern Atlantic and Pacific Oceans, northern polar regions
page 22	**plover**	length 9 in (23 cm)	insects, worms, other invertebrates	worldwide except for polar regions and the Sahara
page 23	**maleo**	length 23 in (58 cm)	fruit, seeds, mollusks, insects, other small invertebrates	Indonesia
pages 23, 34	**emperor penguin**	height 45 in (114 cm)	krill, fish, squid	Antarctica
pages 24, 35	**peregrine falcon**	length 17 in (43 cm)	birds, small mammals, reptiles, insects	temperate regions worldwide as well as urban enviroments
page 24	**secretary bird**	height 4½ ft (137 cm)	small mammals, reptiles, birds, insects	central and southern Africa
page 24	**American white pelican**	wingspan 9 ft (274 cm)	fish, crayfish, amphibians	North America
page 25	**golden eagle**	length 35 in (89 cm) wingspan 7 ft (213 cm)	mammals, birds, carrion	much of North America, Europe, and Asia except for polar regions
page 25	**barred owl**	wingspan 44 in (112 cm)	small mammals, birds, amphibians, reptiles, insects	North America
page 26	**European roller**	length 1 ft (30 cm)	insects, small reptiles, rodents, frogs	Europe, Middle East, central Asia, Morocco
page 26	**potoo**	length 15 in (38 cm)	insects	southern Central America, northern and central South America
page 26	**hooded pitohui**	length 9 in (23 cm)	fruit, seeds, invertebrates	New Guinea
page 27	**hoopoe**	length 10 in (25 cm)	insects, small reptiles, frogs, seeds, berries	Africa, Asia, Europe
page 27	**Australian magpie**	wingspan 29 in (74 cm)	small animals, insects, seeds, nuts, fruit	Australia, New Guinea, Tasmania, New Zealand
page 27	**killdeer**	length 9 in (23 cm)	insects, other invertebrates	North America, West Indies, Peru
page 27	**burrowing owl**	length 9 in (23 cm)	insects, small mammals	North and South America
page 28	**steamer duck**	length 29 in (74 cm)	shellfish, aquatic invertebrates	South America
page 28	**greater rhea**	height 5 ft (152 cm) weight 65 lbs (29 kg)	plants, fruit, seeds, insects, small reptiles, rodents	South America
page 29	**northern gannet**	length 37 in (94 cm)	small fish, squid	Atlantic Ocean, Western Europe, northeastern North America
page 29	**mallard**	length 2 ft (61 cm)	seeds, acorns, berries, plants, insects, shellfish	most temperate and subtropical regions worldwide
page 29	**Humboldt penguin**	length 25 in (64 cm)	fish	coasts of Chile and Peru
page 30	**rock pigeon**	length 13 in (33 cm)	in the wild: seeds, fruit, insects	originally Europe, North Africa, Asia; now found in cities worldwide
page 31	**arctic tern**	length 13 in (33 cm)	small fish, crustaceans	polar regions

	name	size	diet	range
page 32	**marabou stork**	height 5 ft (1½ m)	carrion, garbage	central and southern Africa
page 32	**cassowary**	height 5 ft (1½ m)	fruit, plants, invertebrates, small vertebrates	Australia, New Guinea
page 33	**red bird of paradise**	length 1 ft (30 cm)	fruit, spiders	Indonesia
page 34	**Rüppell's vulture**	length 38 in (97 cm)	carrion	North Africa, eastern Africa
page 35	**wandering albatross**	wingspan 10 ft (3 m)	squid, small fish, crustaceans	oceans worldwide except the North Atlantic
page 35	**kori bustard**	length 4 ft (122 cm)	insects, small mammals, reptiles, seeds, berries, carrion	eastern and southern Africa
page 35	**red-billed quelea**	length 4½ in (11 cm)	seeds, cereal crops	central and southern Africa
page 35	**pink cockatoo**	length 14 in (36 cm)	grasses, plants, insect larvae	Australia
page 36	**kākāpō**	length 2 ft (61 cm)	plants, seeds, fruit, pollen	New Zealand
page 36	**northern bald ibis**	length 30 in (76 cm)	lizards, small mammals, birds, invertebrates	southern Morocco
page 36	**California condor**	wingspan 9 ft (274 cm)	carrion, small mammals, fish	southwestern United States and Mexico
page 36	**blue-throated macaw**	length 33 in (84 cm)	palm fruit	north-central Bolivia
page 37	**passenger pigeon**	length 16 in (41 cm)	nuts, berries, invertebrates	North America
page 37	**dodo**	height 3 ft (91 cm)	fruit, nuts, seeds, bulbs, roots	Mauritius
page 37	**ivory-billed woodpecker**	length 20 in (51 cm)	larvae, fruit, nuts, seeds	southern United States and Cuba
page 37	**elephant bird**	height 10 ft (3 m)	probably fruit, other plant materials	Madagascar
page 37	**whooping crane**	wingspan 7 ft (213 cm)	crustaceans, mollusks, fish, small reptiles, aquatic plants	North America

For more information:

Books

The Big Book of Birds. By Yuval Zommer. Thames & Hudson, 2019.

Bird: The Definitive Visual Guide. Edited by Janashree Singha. DK, Penguin Random House, 2019.

Egg & Nest. By Rosamond Purcell, Linnea S. Hall, René Corado. The Belknap Press of Harvard University Press, 2008.

The Life of Birds. By David Attenborough. Princeton University Press, 1998.

The Sibley Guide to Birds. By David Allen Sibley. Alfred A. Knopf, 2000.

Weird Birds. By Chris Earley. Firefly Books, 2014.

What Is a Bird? Edited by Tony D. Williams. Princeton University Press, 2020.

Websites

Birds of the World
birdsoftheworld.org

British Broadcasting Corporation
bbc.co.uk/programmes/b007qn69

Defenders of Wildlife
defenders.org/wildlife/california-condor

LiveScience
livescience.com/search?searchTerm=bird+facts

National Audubon Society
audubon.org

National Geographic
nationalgeographic.com